1

£1.00

GW00889428

Hidc

Dorset

by Robert Westwood

Inspiring Places Publishing
2 Down Lodge Close
Alderholt
Fordingbriidge
SP6 3JA
ISBN 978-0-8384668-0-0
© Robert Westwood 2021

Contains Ordnance Survey data © Crown copyright and database right (2011)

JURASSICCOAST
**QUALITY
BUSINESS**

2

Contents

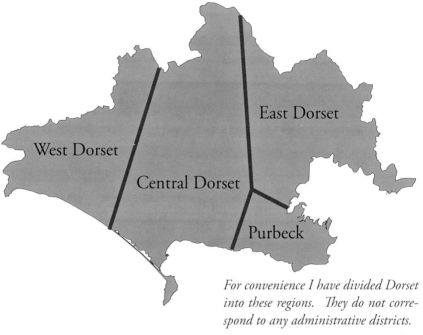

East Dorset

West Dorset

Central Dorset

Purbeck

For convenience I have divided Dorset into these regions. They do not correspond to any administrative districts.

Milton Abbey and school (page 22).

Introduction

In 2018 over three million tourists paid a staying visit to Dorset. Coastal resorts such as Bournemouth, Weymouth, Swanage and Lyme Regis have lots to offer the visitor, as do beauty spots such as Durdle Door and historic sites like Corfe Castle. These places are often busy, especially in the school holidays and some may feel the need to escape the 'madding crowd' and seek interest, beauty and tranquility in less visited locations. If you fit this category, whether for a day or two, or longer, this book is for you. It's not as difficult as you may think, over forty per cent of Dorset is designated as an Area of Outstanding Natural Beauty with picturesque villages and historic sites scattered throughout; many accessed by quiet country roads and footpaths. There are spectacular viewpoints where you can enjoy a picnic, walk the dog or simply relax and wander. There are enigmatic ruins to explore and even stretches of Dorset's marvellous Jurassic Coast where you can escape the crowds. Of course, many of the places mentioned in this book do attract visitors, but they are all relatively quiet, even in the busiest holiday times, and are generally much less well-known than the major tourist centres and attractions. If you want to make the most of a visit to Dorset I would strongly recommend you take the time to explore at least some of 'Hidden Dorset'.

Finding your way

I have included details of the places featured and how to access them, and have also suggested a few walks in quiet and beautiful locations. Six figure grid references are used as well as postcodes – sometimes the latter are the nearest available. I have also occasionally used what3words when appropriate. Forgive me if you are aware of this facility already but I thought it best to provide some guidance for those who may not yet be familiar with it.

what3words

This is a sophisticated algorithm which allocates a unique three word code for anywhere on the planet, to an accuracy of three metres squared. An example is count.swordfish.observer which I have used to locate Winspit on the Isle of Purbeck. You will need a smartphone and will have to download the what3words app (free). As well as giving your present position, you can search for a location and then navigate there via google or apple maps. You may not find yourself in the exact three metre square that the words define but the maps may indicate you are only a few metres away, which should enable you to confirm your position.

I would always recommend using Ordnance Survey Explorer maps in addition to electronic means of navigation. Sheets 116,117,118,129 and OL15 will cover the county.

East Dorset

Historic Sites

Cranborne is a small village on the edge of the 'Chase' to which it gives its name and which came into being as a royal hunting ground. Once a favourite with King John, it developed into an important administrative centre and garrison town. Henry VIII built a hunting lodge which was remodelled in the early seventeenth century by Robert Cecil, 1st Earl of Salisbury, into the beautiful manor house we see today. The manor stands on the site of Cranborne Abbey; founded in the tenth century. It is not open to the public but good views of it are to be had from the B3081 as it leaves Cranborne and particularly from the footpaths bordering the north side of the grounds where a notice charmingly tells visitors they are free to wander over the land and picnic if they wish. On Wednesdays in summer the lovely gardens bordering the manor are open.

On the eastern side of Cranborne, just as the B3078 enters the village, Castle Hill Lane leads up to the site of **Cranborne Castle**. This was a motte and bailey castle, one of many built by the Normans in the years following the Conquest. Nothing now remains of the building, probably just a wooden structure, but the hill or motte still stands and it is a lovely place to explore, especially in early summer when the bluebells and wild garlic are out.

Cranborne has two pubs and a restaurant plus a tea room at the garden centre. The "Fleur de Lys" featured as the "Flower-de-Luce" in Thomas Hardy's *Tess of the d'Urbervilles* and was where, one Saturday night, Tess

Cranborne Castle.

fatefully accepted a lift home from Alec d'Urberville.

A few miles out of Cranborne, this time westwards along the B3081, you will find the best preserved Roman road in southern Britain. Just before the roundabout on the A354 you can clearly see the straight bank, known as **Ackling Dyke** stretching away either side of the road. You are free to walk along the Roman road in either direction.

Bokerley Dyke is a linear earthwork on the Dorset / Hampshire border. Dating from the Bronze Age it was remodelled in around 350 AD, prompting speculation that it formed some sort of defensive line for the Romano-British people against the threat of invasion from the Saxons. It overlooks Martin Down, a remarkable slice of ancient Chalk downland. There are many paths to wander and the setting is superb.

On the edge of the Chalk escarpment and with wonderful views over the valley of the River Stour, **Hambledon** (picture page 10,11)**and Hod Hill** (below) are two spectacular Iron Age hillforts. Both are easily accessed and you are free to wander around. Hambledon was originally the site of a Neolithic causewayed camp and was later developed by Iron Age inhabitants into a stronghold. Their ramparts are particularly impressive on the western side of the hill. During the English Civil War the hill was the scene of con-

Bokerley Dyke.

Hod Hill viewed from Hambledon Hill.

frontation between the Dorset Club-men, a group of locals fed up with constant war, and the forces of Parliament. They were quickly dealt with by Oliver Cromwell, who held prisoners overnight in the nearby church at Shroton.

Hod Hill seems to have developed later as an Iron Age hillfort than Hambledon and also has impressive ramparts. The Romans built a fort in the north-western corner after they had captured it. Excavations have shown a concentration of Roman ballista catapult bolts in and around the site of one particular Iron Age hut and it has been speculated that they targeted the home of the local chieftain.

Another hillfort is **Badbury Rings** near Wimborne. Looked after by the National Trust, it too has great views and a lovely, wooded summit. On the way there you can marvel at the beautiful avenue of beech trees on the B3082.

Picturesque Villages

The Tarrant is a delightful twelve mile long tributary of the River Stour. A

Badbury Rings.

Badbury Rings.

typical Chalk stream, its name derives from the Celtic word meaning "trespasser", presumably because of its frequent deviations from its narrow channel. Along this lovely valley are eight villages all bearing the name of the river and all, apart from Tarrant Launceston, with a pretty, medieval church. There are many footpaths to please walkers and a couple of sites that are worth a visit in their own right. At **Tarrant Rushton** an old airfield has now returned to farmland. This was the place where, on the night of June 5/6th 1944, gliders took off for Normandy to land the first troops in Operation Overlord. There is a simple memorial near the entrance and a huge hangar remains; you

The old airfield, Tarrant Rushton.

Ashmore.

can walk along the old perimeter road.

At **Tarrant Crawford** an ancient church is all that remains of a once prosperous Cistercian nunnery. The churchyard is said to hold the grave of Queen Joan of Scotland, daughter of King John and, according to one legend, buried in a gold coffin. It is a charming location and there are some interesting medieval wall paintings in the church.

One of the highest villages in Dorset, **Ashmore** sits at the north-eastern corner of Cranborne Chase. Such villages, high up on the permeable Chalk, have traditionally had problems with water supply and Ashmore famously retains its "Dew Pond" which only very rarely dries out. The pond is a hollow lined with clay and relies simply on rainwater to keep it replenished. It creates a particularly picturesque centre to this quiet, out of the way settlement. On June 24th, Midsummers Day, Ashmore holds the Filly Loo festival. This started in 1956 and is based on the an-

cient custom of baking and eating cakes around the pond on the rare occasions when it dried out. Today the festival involves processions and dancing and has become quite a tourist attraction.

Near Ashmore and also on the edge of the Chalk upland is **Compton Abbas Airfield**, perhaps the most

Compton Abbas Airfield.

Tarrant Crawford Church.

picturesque airfield in the country and one which positively encourages visitors to come and enjoy the setting and the comings and goings of the small aircraft. There is a cafe and outside terrace where everyone is welcome and it is a great spot for lunch or afternoon tea.

Idyllic, Tranquil Places

A few miles along the B3078 from Cranborne to Wimborne lies **Knowlton Church**. Many regard this as a special place, a ruined medieval church set inside a Neolithic henge constructed over four thousand years ago. Nearby were other henges whose outlines can be seen from the air and it is likely that this was a major religious and ceremonial centre in Neolithic and Bronze Age times. The largest burial barrow in Dorset sits a few yards away to the east. It is a beautiful and atmospheric spot; go late on a

summer's evening and you will not be disappointed.

A Beautiful, Quiet Walk

This walk begins and ends in Cranborne. Follow the minor road north-west out of the village square and fork left along a small tarmac road as the 'main' road swings right (1). This soon turns into a rough track; follow it all the way the top, ignoring paths on your left and a stile on your right. You will come to a gate - go through and keep straight on ignoring a path to your left. You'll soon arrive at Penbury Knoll (2), yet another hillfort, but this time a smaller, more intimate one. There are lovely views all around, northwards over the village of Pentridge, "Trantridge" in Thomas Hardy's *Tess of the D'Urbervilles*. The path you will have taken is part of the Hardy Way and is the route taken by

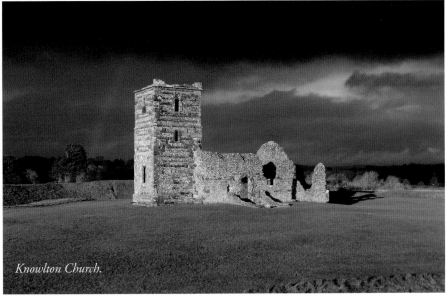

Knowlton Church.

9

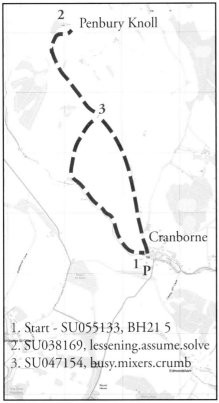

2 Penbury Knoll

3

Cranborne

1 P

1. Start - SU055133, BH21 5
2. SU038169, lessening.assume.solve
3. SU047154, busy.mixers.crumb

Tess on a fateful night after she has par-
tied in "Chaseborough" (Cranborne) at
the "Flower de Luce" (the Fleur de Lys).

Return the same way but turn
right at "Jack's Hedge Corner" (3)
which you will have passed on the way
up. Follow this path downhill, turn left
at the farm and you will arrive back in
Cranborne near the beautiful manor.

Penbury Knoll.

Pentridge from Penbury Knoll.

Special Place - Hambledon Hill

Before Iron Age people built a hillfort here, Neolithic folk had constructed a 'causewayed camp'. This may have been some sort of ceremonial meeting place rather than a defensive structure; there is possibly evidence of feasting here.

Getting there: See page 12.

Dog walking

This is a great place to run your dog but be aware that there may be livestock grazing so please follow all instructions. (Ronnie loves it!)

Picnicking

You'll have to carry the picnic up a steep hill but the views are worth it! Sit on the north-western side (illustrated) on the impressive ramparts. It's best in late afternoon or evening when the sun is low in the sky.

Locations

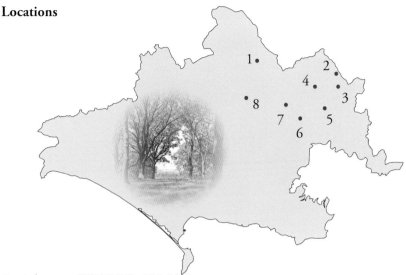

1 - Ashmore, ST912178, SP5 5AF.
Compton Abbas Airfield, ST894186, SP7 0DT.
2 - Bokerley Dyke, SU057191, SP6 3LB. There is a small car park at the end of Sillens Lane in the village of Martin.
3 - Cranborne, SU054135, BH21 5PU.
4 - Ackling Dyke, SU018167, SP5 5QP. It is usually possible to park on the B3081 near the dyke.
5 - Knowlton Church, SU023102, BH21 5LT. About 2.5 miles south of Cranborne on the B3078 take the small road to Wimborne St Giles and Brockington. You can park near the church.
6 - Badbury Rings, ST962031, BH21 4DZ.
7- Tarrant Rushton Airfield, ST949061, DT11 8RZ.
8 - Hambledon Hill, ST853112, DT11 8PS.

Places to Eat and Drink
The Fleur de Lys and the *Sheaf of Arrows* at Cranborne. The cafe at the garden centre is also popular.
Sit and watch the aircraft in or outside the cafe at Compton Abbas Airfield.
The *Horton Inn* is very close to Knowlton Church (BH21 5AD).
The True Lovers' Knot (DT11 9JG) is very near Badbury Rings and Tarrant Rushton.
Wimborne has many pubs, restaurants and cafes.

Cranborne Manor

Purbeck

The Purbeck Coast

While Swanage, Kimmeridge, Lulworth and Durdle Door attract thousands of visitors, there are many other beautiful and fascinating places on the coast of Purbeck. These are not exactly unknown, but they are all less frequented and places where you can relax and enjoy the scenery in peace. Typically they require a little effort on foot to get there.

When the army ranges are open the coast path east of Lulworth follows a dramatic course above the famous Fossil Forest before reaching **Mupe Bay** (see page 16). It is possible to walk/scramble down to the beach and even in the summer you may have it all to yourself. You may see a yacht anchored offshore as many sailors know what a beautiful, secluded spot this is.

Many quarries once worked the Portland Stone along Purbeck's southern shore and two of these, **Seacombe** and **Winspit**, are great places to scramble around, sit and relax, and enjoy the sound of the waves on the rocks. Both are easily accessed from Worth Matravers and of the two, Winspit is probably the most well-known and attracts most visitors. Winspit was active well into the twentieth century and has vast caves excavated by the quarrymen as well as wonderful views along the Purbeck coast.

A shortish, level walk from the small car park on the edge of Kingston will take you to the coast at **Houns-tout**. This high cliff, capped by Portland and Purbeck limestone, provides stunning views east along the Jurassic Coast and west across **Chapman's Pool** and **St Aldhelm's Head**. You can walk down to

Chapman's Pool.

Corfe Common.

St Aldhelm's Chapel.

St Aldhelm's Chapel.

Chapman's Pool where, again, you may have the beach all to yourself. There is no need to walk back up the steep climb to Houns-tout, you can follow the wooded valley to Hill Bottom and from there take the path to Kingston.

St Aldhelm's Head can also be reached from Worth Matravers. Here, again, are wonderful views. There is also a small, Norman chapel dedicated to St Aldhelm, probably on the site of a much older church. The stainless steel sculpture on the headland is a memorial to the development of radar here during the Second World War.

At the other end of Purbeck and on the rim of Poole Harbour is **Shipstal Point**. This is a short walk over the

heathland from the RSPB car park at Arne. Another lovely, secluded spot, there is a small sandy beach and the water is almost invariably calm.

Historic Sites

A quiet little village at the northern end of Purbeck, **Moreton** boasts a tranquil setting by the River Frome, a charming tea room, the grave of Lawrence of Arabia and a wonderful church. From the outside you may not think the church of St Nicholas remarkable, but look closely at the windows. The church was unluckily damaged by a stray bomb jettisoned by a returning German bomber in World War II. The building was repaired and the original stained glass windows were replaced by ones engraved by Laurence Whistler. The effect is dramatic and the inside of the church has been transformed. The church held the funeral service of Lawrence of Arabia, whose simple cottage is on nearby Clouds Hill, and his grave is in the "new" churchyard across the road. Tucked away in Purbeck's central valley just west of Church Knowle is the tiny village of **Steeple**; just a few houses and the charming church of **St Michael**. Carved on the wall of the porch is the coat of arms of the Washington family who had married into the local, wealthy Lawrence family. The first US president, George Washington, was a great grandson of John Washington of Steeple who had moved to Virginia. It is said that George Washington took inspiration for the US flag from the coat of arms on his signet ring which features stars and stripes.

Idyllic, Tranquil Places

There are plenty of idyllic places in Purbeck, but some can be far from tranquil in the holiday season. That shouldn't put you off visiting however and below are a few places that are never overwhelmed by the number of visitors.

Kingston is a small village a short distance from Corfe Castle. It boasts quaint cottages of Purbeck Stone, a pub with spectacular views and a wonderful Victorian church. Follow the road past the church and you will find the free Houns-tout car park. From here a good level path leads to Houns-tout cliff with amazing views east and west along the Jurassic Coast. The walk takes around half an hour each way and is the perfect preparation for a visit to the Scott Arms afterwards.

The walk follows the eastern edge of the 'Golden Valley' with views over the Encombe estate and glimpses of the splendid Encombe House. Just over the other side of the Golden Valley is Swyre Head which arguably offers the best views anywhere in Purbeck (see walk page 16, picture pages 18,19).

Corfe Castle is undoubtedly idyllic but seldom tranquil and one of the least 'secret' places in the whole of Dorset. However, follow West Street from the Square to the end and you will arrive at **Corfe Common.** This is typically quiet and uncrowded and you are

A detail from a window, Moreton Church.

Kingston Church.

free to wander, run the dog and, from almost everywhere, enjoy lovely views of the castle and village.

A Beautiful, Quiet Walk

You can start from Kingston if you wish or park at Sheeps Pen Car Park at the end of the road westwards out of the village (carry on past the pub and church). From here go through the gate and follow the grassy path up and across the field. Keep the woods to your right and you will soon arrive at Swyre Head from where the views east and west along the coast are amazing (see pages 18,19). When you're ready walk north-eastwards along by the wall on the far side and go through a gate. Immediately turn right along a path that leads back to the car park and Kingston.

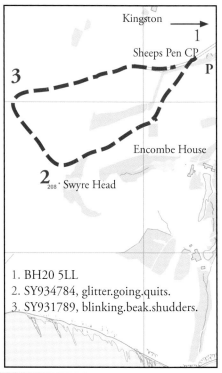

1. BH20 5LL
2. SY934784, glitter.going.quits.
3. SY931789, blinking.beak.shudders.

Mupe Bay.

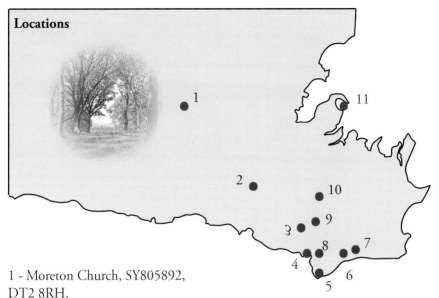

Locations

1 - Moreton Church, SY805892, DT2 8RH.

2 - Steeple Church, SY911808, BH20 5NY.

3 - Sheeps Pen car park (for Swyre Head), SY933784, BH20 5LL.

4 - Houns-tout, SY950773, BH20 5ED, Houns-tout car park, SY953794, BH20 5LL, riverside.witty.origins.

5 - St Aldhelm's Head, SY960754, BH19 3LR, Renscombe car park, SY964771, BH19 3LL, sway.tubes.flesh.

6 - Winspit, SY976760, count.swordfish.observer.

7 - Seacombe, SY984766, equivocal.bonds.harps.

8 - Chapman's Pool, see 4 above.

9 - Kingston - see Houns-tout car park above, 4 and *Scott Arms*.

10 - Corfe Common, SY958813, defenders.pancake.likewise.

11 - Shipstal Point, SY982884, flies.cups.report, car park, SY972881, BH20 5BJ.

Places to Eat and Drink

The Square and Compass at Worth Matravers (BH19 3LF) is charming, rustic but also quite popular. Equally delightful in Worth is the *Worth Matravers Tea and Supper Room* which is on the square just down from the pub.

The Scott Arms in Kingston (BH20 5LH) has wonderful views of Corfe Castle.

The Dovecote Cafe is in 'The Walled Garden' at Moreton, very near the church.

The New Inn is in the picturesque village of Church Knowle a few miles from Corfe Castle, BH20 5NQ.

The Seventh Wave Restaurant on Durlston Head has fantastic sea views, BH19 2JL.

Shipstal Point.

Special Place - Swyre Head

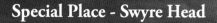

Swyre Head is a wonderful promontory on the ridge of Purbeck limestone with amazing views both east and west over the Jurassic Coast. This is the view westwards with Kimmeridge bay in the middle of the picture and Clavell Tower to the left. Beyond Kimmeridge you can see the impressive Gad Cliff with its dipping layers of Portland and Purbeck limestone. Hidden from view behind Gad Cliff is Worbarrow Bay.

Dog walking

A good walk for them from Sheeps Pen Car Park (see page 16 and Locations). Keep on a lead if cattle or sheep. Usually safe to run around on Swyre Head.

Picnicking

A good spot if you don't mind carrying from the car park. There's a central mound with a seat that has views all round.

Central Dorset

Historic Sites

Cerne Abbas lies in a beautiful valley cut into the northern edge of the Chalk downland. This fertile vale has been inhabited since prehistoric times and is in an Area of Outstanding Natural Beauty. The village is well-known with many visitors stopping by to see the famous Giant, a 180 feet high figure cut into the hillside and whose age is still debated. Some think it ancient, perhaps representing Hercules since he holds a large club, but there is no mention of it before the seventeenth century and some think it is a caricature of Oliver Cromwell. You may wonder how this famous figure fits in with secret Dorset – well, many visitors fail to find the village's real gems. At

The Abbot's Porch, Cerne Abbey.

the end of the street by the church is Abbey Farm where visitors are allowed (a small donation is requested) to view the remains of the Benedictine abbey which was founded in 987 AD. The remains are meagre but charming; both the **Abbot's Porch** and the **Guesthouse** date from the fifteenth century. Nearby is a peaceful churchyard with, at the far corner, the **Silver Well**. This lovely spot is a Chalk spring and is reputedly the spot where St Augustine struck the ground with his staff after asking local shepherds if their thirst would be better quenched by beer or water. The spring flowed as a response to their pious reply. However, it owes its name to the more likely and charming story that it is the place where St Edwold, a Saxon nobleman tired of constant warfare, lived as a hermit. He asked the locals where to find water and rewarded them with silver coins when they showed him the spring. Dipping a new born baby as the first rays of the sun strike the water is said to bring health and happiness.

Head north from Cerne Abbas along the A352 and you will shortly reach the little village of **Minterne Magna**. Here is the imposing home

The Silver Well.

Minterne Gardens.

of the Churchill and Digby families with gardens open to the public and especially beautiful in May when the azaleas and rhododendrons are out. Just north of the village a road to the left leads along the top of the Chalk escarpment with, after a while, wonderful views over the Vale of Blackmore, Thomas Hardy's "Vale of Little Dairies". By the side of the road is a small enigmatic stone pillar, known as the "**Cross in Hand**". This may have been an ancient boundary marker but in his poem "The Lost Pyx" Thomas Hardy recounts a more interesting origin. Journeying to deliver the last rites to an old shepherd on a stormy night, the local priest lost the silver box (pyx) that held the sacrament. Searching for it, he found the pyx illuminated and with a group of cattle around it. He erected the pillar to mark the spot. It was also the scene in *Tess of the D'Urbervilles* where Alec met Tess and begged her not to tempt him again.

Dorchester is a thriving county town with interesting museums, boutique shops and vibrant bars and bistros. Many, though, will miss some of its fascinating and atmospheric corners. The River Frome skirts its northern edge and the footpath here passes "**Hangman's Cottage**". The name is still on the door of this quaint, private, thatched dwelling and it was formerly the home of the nearby jail's official hangman. If you walked here you probably passed the old jail outside of which sixteen year old Thomas Hardy witnessed the public execution of Martha Brown, reputedly providing the inspiration for the ending of the eponymous heroine of *Tess of the D'Urbervilles*.

A little further on beside the council buildings is the **Roman townhouse** whose expert excavation has revealed a sophisticated ancient home with some beautifully preserved mosaics. Continuing the Roman theme is **Maumbury Rings**, due south

The Roman aqueduct, Poundbury.

and next to Dorchester South station. This was a Neolithic site that became a Roman amphitheatre.

Finally, at the north-western edge of the town on Poundbury Road is **Poundbury hillfort**. This is a lovely spot to wander around and the ramparts of the Iron Age hillfort are still impressive. On the northern side of the hill it is possible to see the course of the Roman aqueduct which was a remarkable piece of engineering built to provide the town with water.

Idyllic, Tranquil Places

Bulbarrow Hill is one of a number of viewpoints on the edge of the Chalk escarpment with views over the Vale of Blackmore, a scene famously described by Thomas Hardy in *Tess of the D'Urbervilles* and in his poem "Wessex Heights". At the western edge of the hill sits Rawlsbury Camp (see pages 30,31). This hillfort is easily accessed via a short footpath; it offers stunning views and is a perfect place for a picnic.

The small intimate valleys that cut the Chalk to the south of Bulbarrow hide a number of "secret" spots that will delight the visitor. The village of **Milton Abbas** is quite well-known; it was built in the late eighteenth century by the local landowner who didn't like the proximity to his grand house of the original village. The long street with its identical thatched cottages is much photographed. Perhaps less visited is **Milton Abbey**; although part of a public school, visitors are welcome to view the abbey and a path leads to St Catherine's Chapel, once reached by a unique line of grass steps. The view from the chapel is lovely.

A little west of Milton Abbas lie the villages of **Lower Ansty** and **Melcombe Bingham** from where a number of relatively short paths lead up to the "**Dorsetshire Gap**", a charmingly named saddle in the Chalk escarpment. Some regard this as the very heart of Dorset and the views certainly reflect the visions of rural beauty and tranquility with which the county is often associated. The even more charmingly named **Bingham's Melcombe** presents a near perfect vision of rural idyll. Although the lovely manor is private, it is possible to walk to the adjacent fourteenth century church of St Andrew, passing the beautiful house on the way.

Milton Abbey.

Valley of Stones.

White Nothe (photo page 25) arguably offers the best views anywhere on the Jurassic Coast. Eastwards you look across the Chalk cliffs to Bat's Head with the limestone headland of St Aldhelm's in the distance, while westwards Ringstead Bay, Osmington Mills, Weymouth and the Isle of Portland stretch before you. You can reach White Nothe from the National Trust Ringstead car park, a short, easy walk of about twenty minutes. Near the headland is a row of isolated cottages, once Coastguard cottages from the days when their job was primarily to catch and deter smugglers. A steep, windy track, signed the "Smugglers' Path" leads down to the shore from the top of the cliff and featured in J. Meade Faulkner's *Moonfleet*.

A short distance from the village of Portesham is a small nature reserve known as **The Valley of Stones**. The stones are sarsen stones from a hard, silicified layer of sands and gravels lying on top of the Chalk. The layer was

Melcombe Bingham.

broken up by a freeze/thaw action in the last ice age which also led to material slipping downhill; a process known as solifluction. Prehistoric people used these sarsen stones in various monuments. The valley is a beautiful, peaceful spot with footpaths through it.

The Hardy Monument was built to honour Dorset's other Thomas Hardy, the naval hero who was Nelson's Flag Captain at Trafalgar. He was born in the nearby village of Portesham. The views are impressive and the monument served as a marker for shipping off Weymouth; its shape was intended to mimic a naval telescope. Just to the south-east of the monument is **Bronkham Hill**, along which the South Dorset Ridge-

way runs. A walk along here is well worthwhile, the surrounding countryside is lovely and the ridge has many Bronze Age burial barrows.

Several pretty valleys cut the Chalk downs while footpaths along the spurs offer stunning views. One such path offers the chance to see **The Grey Mare and Her Colts**, a chambered Neolithic long barrow and the **Kingston Russell Stone Circle**. The South Dorset Ridgeway continues west of the Hardy Monument and passes near the **Hell Stone**, another long barrow and eventually reaches **Abbotsbury Castle**, an impressive Iron Age hillfort with lovely views over Chesil Beach and the Fleet.

Barrows on Bronkham Hill.

Abbotsbury Castle.

Church Ope Cove.

The Isle of Portland

The people of Portland have traditionally considered themselves different from the rest of Dorset. Tenuously connected to the "mainland" by Chesil Beach, Portland does feel to have a character all its own. Thomas Hardy called it the "Isle of Slingers", a reference to the fact that the ancient Celts used the smooth, rounded pebbles from Chesil Beach as ideal ammunition for their slings. Portland, of course, is famous for its stone, a hard Jurassic limestone that is perfect for monumental structures. It has been quarried since Roman times and is still in demand, although most of the quarries are no longer worked. Unlike its near neighbour Weymouth, Portland is not a major tourist destination but Portland Bill with its lighthouse still draws many visitors.

There are, however, one or two places that fit perfectly with the aims of this book. **Church Ope Cove** sits midway down the east coast of the isle just south of Easton and is reached via a steep line of steps from a path by the charming Portland Museum. Guarding it are the ruins of Rufus Castle, reputedly built for William Rufus (William II) although the present structure dates from the fifteenth century. Also overlooking the cove and reached by a short path are the ruins of **St Andrew's Church**. This was the first parish church on Portland and was the site of an early Saxon church. It was abandoned in the eighteenth century after a landslip made it unsafe. It is now a lovely spot with fine views out to sea. In the graveyard is a very unusual gravestone; instead of a cross the emblem it carries is a skull and crossbones. In fact several tombs and

White Nothe.

graves have this design but, perhaps disappointingly, it does not mean pirates were buried here, it was simply used to represent man's mortality.

Church Ope Cove itself has a rocky, pebbly beach and is one of the few places on Portland where it is safe and easy to swim off, although only within the cove. There is a lovely coastal path to the south leading to Portland Bill.

Some of Portland's quarries offer opportunities to walk and explore. In particular **Tout Quarry Sculpture Park** in the north-west corner of the isle has many sculptures in its meandering forty acre site as well as great views over Chesil Beach and the Jurassic Coast.

Picturesque Villages

Cerne Abbas and Milton Abbas have already been mentioned, and there are many other lovely villages in central Dorset but here are a few personal favourites.

The Valley of Stones is the head of the valley of the River Bride which

Bride House.

Tout Quarry.

Lower Bockhampton.

Bride Park.

rises a little way down, shortly before it passes through the village of **Little Bredy** (sometimes written **Littlebredy**). This is a pretty estate village with the elegant and picturesque Bride House at its centre and next to a lovely Victorian church. In the valley below the house the River Bredy has been dammed and a small waterfall created, all set in beautiful parkland. Charmingly, the public are free to wander and picnic in this parkland; it is accessed via a path next to the church.

  Lower Bockhampton and neighbouring **Stinsford** have strong Thomas Hardy connections; his heart is buried in Stinsford Church and he went to school in Lower Bockhampton. The church is lovely and the bridge over the River Frome is worth the visit on its own. There is a footpath from here along the river to the church (part of the Hardy Way).

  There is nothing much at **Up Cerne** (near Cerne Abbas), but if you're nearby it's worth taking a look at the lovely manor house in a picture-book setting by the church. Finally, the village of **Plush** nestles in a secluded valley it shares with a chalk stream. This is another rural idyll in Dorset's chalk upland and a visit here offers the chance to stop at the popular 'Brace of Pheasants'.

Up Cerne Manor.

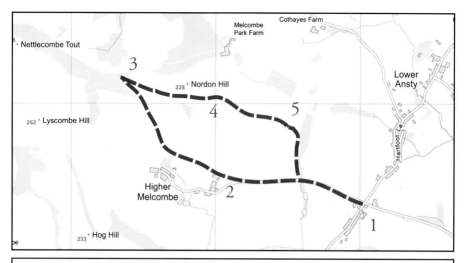

1. Start - ST760023, DT2 7PD. 2. ST751024, cookies.product.resembles
3. ST743031, descended.dignity.sharpness 4. ST750030, sway.unheated.corner
5. ST755026, suitcase.elevated.coping

A Beautiful, Quiet Walk

From Melcombe Bingham take the small road signed "Private road to Higher Melcombe", also marked as a path to the Dorset Gap (1). Just before Higher Melcombe, take a path on the right also signed "Dorset Gap" (2). Follow the bridleway signs and at a fork in the path keep right and head up to the Dorset Gap (3). Several paths meet here, all ancient trackways. Take the path signed "Bulbarrow Hill" heading roughly eastwards. This path is the Wessex Ridgeway; follow it uphill and when you see a stile in front of you, turn right towards the hedge forming the field boundary (4). Follow this path alongside the hedge at the top of the ridge with great views of Higher Melcombe and the deserted medieval village to your right. Keep going until the path starts to descend with a wooded area in front of you (5). Turn right down the hill towards a small brick building, turn left on the road and follow it back to Melcombe Bingham.

Locations
1 - Minterne Magna, ST658043, DT2 7AS.
2 - Up Cerne, ST657028, DT2 7AW.
3 - Cerne Abbas (parking and picnic), ST663016, DT2 7JF.
4 - Dorchester (Acland Road car park), SY693905, DT1 1EA. Maumbury Rings, SY690899, many.reward. enlighten. Roman Town House, SY689909, pushover.dupe.replenish.
5 - Stinsford Church, SY711910, DT2 8PY.
5(also) - Lower Bockhampton, SY720907, DT2 8PZ.
6 - Tout Quarry, SY687727, DT5 2EN.

Locations

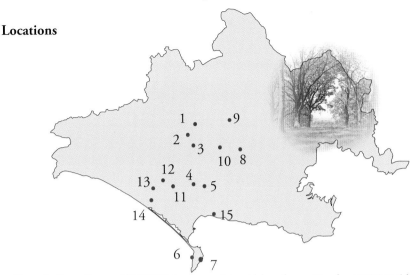

7 - Church Ope Cove - SY697710, DT5 1HT.

8 - Milton Abbas, ST798022, DT11 0AY. Milton Abbey (visitor parking) ST799025.

9 - Rawlsbury Camp, ST769058, DT11 0HE.

10 - Melcombe Bingham, ST760023, DT2 7NZ.

10(also) - Bingham's Melcombe, ST772019, DT2 7NZ (start of footpath by road).

11 - Hardy Monument, SY612876, DT2 9HD.

12 - Littlebredy, road by church, SY588890, DT2 9HN.

12 - Valley of Stones (parking), SY601873, DT2 9HX.

13 - The Grey Mare and Her Colts, SY583870, DT3 4LD, intervene. fluffed.shaver.

13 - Kingston Russell Stone Circle, SY577878, inflict.accordion.prune. Parking at SY588865, mailing.sunroof. grapevine.

14 - Abbotsbury Castle, SY557864, DT2 9BS, fried.fabric.dabbled.

15 - Ringstead Bay (NT car park), SY757824, DT2 8NG.

Places to Eat and Drink

The New Inn, The Giant Inn and The Royal Oak, all in Cerne Abbas, DT2 7AF (The Giant Inn).

The Abbot's Tea Room, also in Cerne Abbas, DT2 7JF.

The Fox at Ansty, DT2 7PD.

The Hambro Arms in Milton Abbas, DT11 0BW.

The Brace of Pheasants in Plush is a popular eating place. DT2 7RQ.

The Lobster Pot at Portland Bill has a great location. DT2 2JT.

Milton Abbas.

Special Place - Rawlsbury Camp

A spur on the Chalk escarpment at Bulbarrow, Rawlsbury Camp is, at around 900 feet, the second highest Iron Age hillfort in Dorset. It has not been excavated so little is known of its ancient past. Views to the north, south and west are simply breathtaking. The main picture looks to the south-west, while inset is the view north over the fertile Blackmore Vale, Thomas Hardy's 'Vale of little dairies'.

Getting there: see page 29.

Dog walking
Just a short footpath from the road.
Keep on lead if cattle grazing.
Picnicking
A good spot and a relatively short
walk to get to the hillfort. Sit on the
top and enjoy the views.

West Dorset

In Lyme Regis and Charmouth west Dorset has two of the county's most popular holiday destinations; but in the rolling countryside of their hinterland there are some delightfully pretty villages and beauty spots. Even near the coast there are some quiet places where you can wander and enjoy spectacular views.

Coney's Castle.

Historic Sites

Powerstock is a small, quaint village a few miles north-east of Bridport. It sits in the steep valley of the Mangerton River and has many pretty cottages, a good pub and a lovely church. This is a beautiful area, just on the edge of the Chalk downs. A little way south-east of the village and carved into the downs, sits **Eggardon Hill** (pages 38,39), another Iron Age hillfort with a magnificent setting. The famous smuggler, Isaac Gulliver, bought a farm here and planted trees on the hill to guide his ships. Eggardon has a number of mysterious legends associated with it including demons, witches and fairies.

Three more of Dorset's Iron Age hillforts are deserving of a mention here. **Lambert's Castle**, neighbouring **Coney's Castle** and nearby **Pilsdon Pen** will all reward a visit. Lambert's Castle is well-known by locals, particularly those with dogs. It is an extensive hillfort with plenty of space to walk and enjoy the wonderful views over the Marshwood Vale from the impressive ramparts. An annual fair was held here from the early eighteenth century until about 1947.

Coney's Castle provides a very different but equally charming experience. It is less than a mile from Lambert's Castle and much smaller. A minor road bisects it and the walking

Whitchurch Canonicorum Church.

St Wite's shrine.

Lambert's Castle.

possibilities are much more limited. However, a stroll along its wooded eastern rampart is enchanting, particularly in spring when it is carpeted with bluebells. **Whitchurch Canonicorum** is a lovely village in the Marshwood Vale and about five miles west of Bridport. It owes its unusual name to Saint Wite (latinised to Saint Candida) whose remains lie in the church. Apart from Westminster Abbey, where the bones of Saint Edward the Confessor lie, this is the only church in Britain with the remains of a saint. Little is known about St Wite, she may have been a Saxon holy woman murdered by marauding Danes, or possibly an anchoress, a type of religious hermit attached to a particular place. A casket inside her shrine in the church is inscribed with words which translate to "Here rest the remains of Saint Wite" and was found to contain the bones of a woman about forty years old. Today the shrine holds many cards asking the saint for help in healing the sick and injured. The church is known as the "Cathedral of the Vale" and was once a place of pilgrimage second only to Canterbury Cathedral.

A very different sort of location is situated just north of Chideock; this is Hell Lane, a sunken lane or "holloway". These features were once ancient cattle droves or perhaps pilgrimage routes and centuries of passing carts and cattle has worn into the soft bedrock, in this case sandstone, and created a miniature gorge. It has a wonderfully atmospheric, somewhat mysterious character and walking along it proves a memorable experience – but dry weather is preferable as part of it becomes a watercourse in wet conditions. It is best accessed from the pretty village of Symondsbury where cottages, church and manor are built of the local, golden limestone.

Idyllic, Tranquil Places

Mapperton House near Beaminster is another built of golden coloured limestone. Its size is perfect for the intimacy of its surroundings and the unusual Italianate garden behind adds to its charm. It seems lost in the rolling hills

Powerstock Common.

of north Dorset and was considered the ideal site for Bathsheba Everdene's farm in the recent Hollywood adaptation of Thomas Hardy's *Far from the Madding Crowd*. It is one of the few places in this book which requires an entrance fee but it is well worth it. You can simply choose to visit the garden or take a tour of the house as well. However, there is no fee to park and enjoy the cafe from where there is a good view of the house and its setting.

Charmouth, just to the east of Lyme Regis, is a popular place to go fossil hunting and the Heritage Centre

there organise walks with experts to show you how and where to look. However, if you simply want to enjoy the beautiful coastal scenery in a quiet setting with opportunity to walk the dog, picnic or just sit and relax, then head up to **Stonebarrow Hill**. At the very eastern end of Charmouth narrow Stonebarrow Lane leads to the large National Trust car park from where there are a variety of lovely walks with far reaching views over the Jurassic Coast. Why not follow the path down to the tiny ruined St Gabriel's Church

Mapperton House.

Stonebarrow.

which once served the now vanished village of Stanton St Gabriel. All that remains is the farmhouse, converted to holiday cottages by the National Trust. From here the energetic can walk up to the summit of Golden Cap and enjoy the spectacular views.

Another lovely and secluded National Trust car park can be found on **Langdon Hill**, just off the A35 between Chideock and Charmouth where a relatively flat walk circles the hill offering wonderful views over coast and countryside as it does so. Like Stonebarrow, this is part of the National Trust's Golden Cap Estate, and again offers a route to the summit of the south coast's highest cliff.

Powerstock Common is a secluded nature reserve managed by the Dorset Wildlife Trust. There are lovely views and many rare and protected plant species. Visit in spring or early summer to make the most of it.

Picturesque Villages

Powerstock and Whitchurch Canonicorum have been mentioned before and both fit into this category. Powerstock has the previously mentioned Common nearby as well as Eggardon Hill (pages 38,39). There are many stone cottages and two good pubs to choose from. **Symondsbury** near Bridport is also charming, has a quaint, welcoming pub and has the unusual sunken track of Hell Lane nearby (page 33).

The Holloway, Symondsbury.

A Beautiful, Quiet Walk

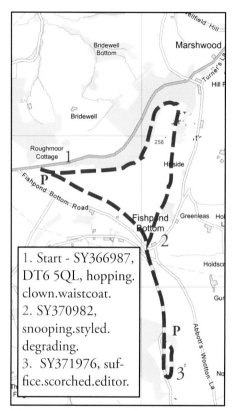

1. Start - SY366987, DT6 5QL, hopping. clown.waistcoat.
2. SY370982, snooping.styled. degrading.
3. SY371976, suffice.scorched.editor.

Colmer's Hill, Symondsbury.

Lambert's Castle.

Coney's Castle.

This is a very easy, short walk. The start (1) is at the large parking area for Lambert's Castle. You are free to wander over this impressive hillfort and I'm suggesting you follow the western edge to the northern end of the fort and then walk back southwards to the southern tip (2). Along this eastern side there are mighty ramparts allowing wonderful views over the Marshwood Vale.

From here take the road going almost due south and then keep left when you come to a junction (Long Lane). This road follows the top of the hill and leads to Coney's Castle. There is a small car park here as well. From the rear of the car park follow the path to the left and walk along the eastern rampart of this small, quaint hillfort. In spring and early summer this wooded glade is full of wild flowers. You can either retrace your steps along the ramparts or walk back along the road when you reach the end (3).

Locations

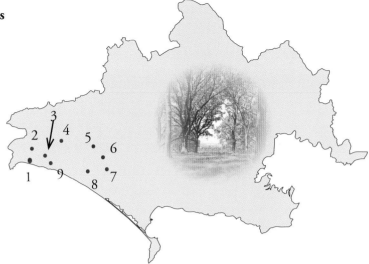

1 - Stonebarrow, Charmouth, SY381932, DT6 6SD.
2 - Lambert's Castle, SY366987, DT6 5QL.
2 - Coney's Castle, SY371976, DT6 6NR.
3 - Whitchurch Canonicorum (church), SY396954, DT6 6RQ.
4 - Pilsdon Pen (parking), ST413009,DT6 5NX.
5 - Mapperton, SY503996, DT8 3NW.
6 - Powerstock Common (parking), SY547973, DT2 0DW.
7 - Eggardon Hill (parking), SY547945, DT6 3ST, homing.thumb.crinkled; entrance, SY545946, chiefs.message.figs.
8 - Symondsbury, SY444936, DT6 6HE; start of 'holloway', SY437937, degrading.mission.amount (follow path along Shute Lane to begin).
9 - Langdon Hill, SY412931, DT6 6JT.

Places to Eat and Drink

The Three Horseshoes, Powerstock, DT6 3TD.
The Marquis of Lorne, Nettlecombe (near Powerstock), DT6 3SY.
The Ilchester Arms, Symondsbury, DT6 6HD.
The Coach House Cafe, Mapperton House, DT8 3NW.
Down House Farm, Higher Eype, near Bridport, DT6 6AH. (This is a beautiful, tranquil spot.)

From Pilsdon Pen.

Special Place - Eggardon Hill

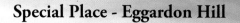

Eggardon Hill (see also page 32) is another of Dorset's spectacular Iron Age hillforts with far reaching views. The southern part of the hill is owned by the National Trust which permits free access throughout the year.

    This hill is composed of hard Cretaceous sands and grits overlying Jurassic sands and clays which form the fertile vale in the distance

Dog walking
Another good spot for walking your dog. Just be aware if cattle are grazing and look out for notices.

Picnicking
A good spot if you don't mind carrying from where you park. The views are amazing.

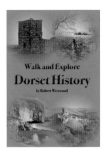

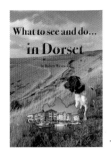

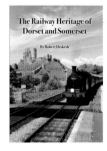

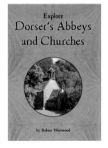

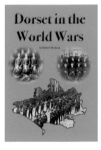

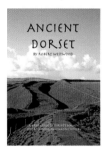

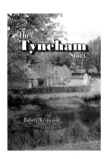

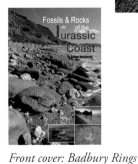

Some more titles by:
Inspiring Places Publishing

A selection of our other titles; for
a full list see - *inspiringplaces.co.uk*

Front cover: Badbury Rings
Rear cover, top: Bride Park, middle: Abbotsbury Abbey, bottom: Knowlton Church.